Essential Norn Irish

About the Author

The late Owen Kelly was one of Northern Ireland's best-loved humorists, known predominantly for his two long-running columns for *The Irish News* – *Kelly's World* and *The Saturday Column*. He was the author of two volumes of autobiography (*Tales Out of School* and *Hens' Teeth*), two volumes of Ulster humour (*Kelly's Country* and *Kelly's World*) and a wealth of newspaper, radio and magazine work. Owen sadly died in 2008.

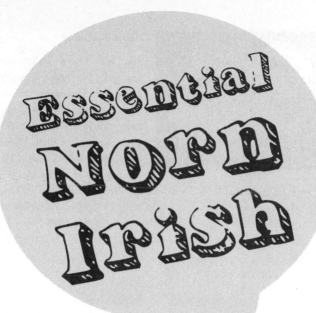

Essential Norn Irish

Yer Man's A to Z Guide to Everyday Banter

Owen Kelly

THE O'BRIEN PRESS
DUBLIN

This edition first published 2016 by
The O'Brien Press Ltd,
12 Terenure Road East, Rathgar, Dublin 6, D06 HD27, Ireland.
Tel: +353 1 4923333; Fax: +353 1 4922777
E-mail: books@obrien.ie. Website: www.obrien.ie
First published 2005 by The Brehon Press Ltd.

The O'Brien Press is a member of Publishing Ireland.

ISBN: 978-1-84717-882-4

1 3 5 7 8 6 4 2
16 18 20 19 17

Printed and bound by Scandbook UAB, Litauen
The paper in this book is produced using pulp from managed forests

Published in

DUBLIN

UNESCO
City of Literature

ABJECT

as in 'I *abject* to your incineration', *meaning* 'I protest at what you imply about me'.

abject may also be a noun, *as in* 'What's that *abject*?', *meaning* 'What is the function of that item?'

ABSOLUTELY

yes.

ABUT

as in '*Abut* that's not what you said yesterday', *meaning* 'I see what you mean but it's at variance with your views of yesterday'.

ACCEPT

as in 'They all went *accept* me', *meaning* 'I didn't accompany the others'.

ACID

as in '*Acid* nigh', *meaning* 'You've got it right'. This applies in various situations, especially in parking a car; **asset** is also used.

AFFLUENT

as in 'It was shakkin, the drains wuz all blacked and the streets wuz full of *affluent*', *meaning* 'The flooding was so severe that the drains backed up and sewage spilled out on the public thoroughfares'.

ANNIE FURDERADOO

imaginary female Norn Iron speaker in whose absence all proceedings begin, *as in* 'Without *Annie Furderadoo* we'll get stuck in'.

ANNIVERSITY

a commemorative date, especially of the matrimonial variety; a composite but obsolete word, combining remembrance and confrontation in equal parts.

ANNOUNCE

as in 'He/she hasn't *announce*', *meaning* 'He/she has no sense of responsibility'.

APPARITION

as in 'He hadda gwin till the hospital for an *apparition*', *meaning* 'His medical condition required surgical intervention'.

ARE

(possessive case) *as in* '*are* house'.

'ARE FAR WART NEVIN'

the opening words of the Lord's Prayer.

ARRISH

adjective describing all matters pertaining to the language, culture and citizenship of **Arland**, especially the Republic of Arland, otherwise known as the Arrish Republic.

ASH IT

exclamation expressing frustration.

Bb

BAIT

as in 'My ma wudda *bait* me round the kitchen', *meaning* 'My mother would have administered corporal punishment had I done that'.

BALD

preparation of an item (usually edible) by prolonging its immersion in hot water: *bald* eggs and *bald* potatoes are examples; *bald* rice is vital to modern cuisine.

BALLY

area of the human anatomy containing the digestive organs.

BAN

as in 'Are youse fer *ban* that or just lukkin?', *meaning* 'Do you intend to purchase that item or are you merely sheltering from the elements?'

BANE

obsolete rural Norn Iron speak for bean.

BAP

as in 'Use yer *bap*', *meaning* 'Think before you act'.

('Down here for dancing' is a more cryptic form of advice, *as in* 'Up here for thinking, down here for dancing'.)

BARD FISH

fish cooked in batter.

BARN

as in 'See ya marra *barn* accidents', *meaning* 'I will meet you tomorrow unless something unforeseen should prevent me from so doing'.

barren is also used on occasion.

BATTER

as in 'Ye *batter* do it', *meaning* 'You would be well advised to comply'.

BATTLE

glass or plastic container for all sorts of liquid, especially alcohol.

BAWD

as in 'I have thee men out *bawd*', *meaning* 'I am unable to start/continue the work at your house because three of my operatives have contracted flu'. *Note:* the operatives and/or the flu may be imaginary.

BECK

as in 'I have a bawd *beck*', *meaning* 'I have hurt my back'. *Note:* this injury is probably fictitious (*see above*).

BEETLE KNOCKERS

as in 'The dactar has me on *beetle knockers*', *meaning* 'My GP has prescribed medication for my high blood pressure'.

BEG

as in 'Thee quid for a wee *beg* of spuds?', *meaning* 'I consider three pounds for a small sack of potatoes to be exorbitant'.

BITE

as in 'What was that all a *bite*?', *meaning* 'What was the cause of that outburst?'

BLACK

concrete object used in building.

BOB

as in 'The place was surrounded with *bob* wire', *meaning* 'A barbed wire fence ensured that there would be no intrusions from uninvited persons'.

BONE ARROW

weapon of choice for one R Hood, Esq, sometime resident of Sherwood Forest, and member of the outlaw class.

BORE

male pig.

BREW

as in 'He was on the *brew* for near a year', *meaning* 'He was out of work for almost twelve months'.

BUNK

as in 'We used to *bunk* aff school', *meaning* 'We used to absent ourselves from lessons without permission'.

Cc

CAP

as in 'what *cap* ye?', *meaning* 'What excuse have you for being so late?'

capped is also used.

CAPS

Police Service of Norn Iron (PSNI).

CAR DOOR

passageway in a building which links various rooms or offices.

CAR KEY

colour, especially of soldier's uniform.

CATTLE

container or device, usually electrical, for heating water.

CHEW

as in 'Stop at *chew*', *meaning* 'Cease that unacceptable behaviour at once'.

If the words are run together, *as in* 'Stopatchew!', there is a hint of retribution in the event of non-compliance.

CHRIS

small slivers of potatoes, fried, salted and sold in various flavours.

CISTERN

as in 'Me *cistern* law gimme that', *meaning* 'That item was a gift from my spouse's sister'.

CLACK

mechanical timekeeping device.

CLAPS

as in 'I said that thing would *claps*', *meaning* 'I predicted that that rickety structure would fall';

also 'I thought I was gonna *claps* wi' the heat', *meaning* 'I feared heat exhaustion'.

CORD

as in 'They nivir even sent me a birthday *cord*', *meaning* 'They didn't bother to mark my birthday in the traditional manner'.

CORNER

public official responsible for establishing that a death might not be due to natural causes, which is frequently the case in Norn Iron; this investigation is referred to as an **ink west**.

COSH

as in 'I paid *cosh*', *meaning* 'I purchased the item with real money as distinct from the cheque, plastic or hire purchase variety'.

Cosh transactions invariably involve sizeable purchases such as cars or even, on occasion, houses.

CRECHE

upper-class Norn Iron speak for, say, the sound of breaking glass or a collision between two or more vehicles.

CRIB

as in 'I crigged me toe on the *crib* pad', *meaning* 'I am in some discomfort as a result of having stubbed my toe on the edge of the pavement'.

CRUSH

collision between two vehicles;

also sound made by falling objects (*see also* **creche**).

CUE

common forename.

CUPOLA

as in 'Gissa *cupola* pints', *meaning* 'Two pints when you have a minute'.

Dd

DAISY

> *as in* 'Take a *daisy*', *meaning* 'Relax'.

DANE

> *as in* 'He was trouble from the *dane* ire I met him', *meaning* 'He created problems for me from the first time we met'.

DEAD-N

> *as in* 'She tuk her *dead-N* at him', *meaning* 'She was highly amused by his antics'.

DEAFENLY

> *as in* 'I *deafenly* dunnit', *meaning* 'You have my word for it: I did exactly as you requested'.

DEE-TEARY-ATE-IT

> *as in* 'Things have *dee-teary-ate-it*', *meaning* 'The situation has worsened'.

DIG

> *as in* 'I gave him a *dig* in the bake', *meaning* 'I struck him on the face';
>
> *also* snide remark.

DORY

> *as in* '*Dory* me', rhyming slang for dough (cash).

DOYLE ERN

> legislative assembly of the Arrish Republic; sometimes simply referred to as the **Doyle**.

DRAWN ROOM

> room in a larger residence where people withdraw after dinner to smoke, scheme and plan devilment.

DUKE

> *as in* 'Take a *duke* at this', *meaning* 'Please let me have your opinion on this';

> *also* the plural, **dukes** (otherwise **Duke of Argylls**), *meaning* painful condition of the rear end of which St. Fiacre, formerly a member of the French nation, is reputed to be the patron saint.

DUN

> *as in* 'I *dun* it', or 'I dunnit', *meaning* 'I have completed the task allotted to me'.

DYNAMITE

as in 'He/she's *dynamite*', which is a tribute to a person's stamina, talent or amorous skills.

Ee

EEL

as in '*Eel* not like that', *meaning* 'That action/ opinion/development will not meet with his approval'.

EFFUSE

as in '*Effuse* too', which is a reciprocal malediction especially prevalent during the marching season.

EGGCUPS

spasmodic inhalation of air.

EGG SIT

the way out.

EIGHT

as in 'Active *eight* at air', *meaning* 'Get that machine going'.

ELAPSE

as in '*Elapse* it up', *meaning* 'He enjoys that entertainment/food/game'.

ELATE

as in '*Elate* anything', *meaning* 'His tastes in food are completely unsophisticated'.

ELECT

as in '*Elect* at', *meaning* 'He enjoyed that experience'.

ELIMINATE

to cast light on; for example: 'We have an outside light to *eliminate* the front door.'

EMERGENCY

as in 'I just put on the *emergency* heater to do the dishes', *meaning* 'I switched on the immersion heater'.

EMMY GRATE

as in 'They all had to *emmy grate*', *meaning* 'For economic reasons they were all forced to go and live in another country'.

ERA

former official name of the Arrish Republic, otherwise known as the Republic of Arland.

ERE

as in 'Am *ere*', *meaning* 'Here I am', *or* 'I have arrived' (*see also* **mere**).

ERRANT

as in 'Ye can get nobody to run an *errant* these days', *meaning* 'No one is willing to go to the corner shop for me'.

EXCEPT

as in 'I can/can't *except* that', *meaning* 'I can/cannot agree to your price/offer'.

EXTRA

as in 'She goes to them *extra* Muriel classes', *meaning* 'She improves her mind, allegedly, by attending evening classes'.

FACILITIES

as in 'He's losing his *facilities*', *meaning* 'His sight and hearing are beginning to deteriorate'.

FAR

male parent; *or* ancient device producing both heat and a means of cooking: a *far* alarm is designed to alert people to the dangers of *far*. Modern *fars* may be powered by gas, electricity or oil. *Far* was a popular weapon in our euphemistically named 'troubles' and many were successfully dealt with by the **farming aid**.

FARMING AID

body of men and women specially trained and equipped to deal with conflagrations.

FASHION

fashion chaps are a universally popular form of fast food, especially after closing time. The delicacy consists of a portion of marine life, deep fried in batter, accompanied by slices of the national vegetable (also fried), both components being laden with calories. *Fashion* is also a riverbank activity, requiring rod, line, bait and patience.

FATE

as in 'Al see ye at ha *fate*', *meaning* 'I will meet you at half past eight'. This may be either am or pm.

FAWN

cooling device, usually electrically powered.

FAX

true details of any situation. 'Get yer *fax* right!' is a frequent exhortation in disputes.

FEW

as in '*Few* don't I will', *meaning* 'If you don't exercise that option, I most certainly will'.

FINE

to discover.

FITS

as in 'He had us in *fits*', *meaning* 'He was most entertaining'.

FLAN

> genteel expletive *as in* 'I'll break your *flan* neck', *meaning* 'I will administer corporal punishment'.

FLAP

> *as in* 'I'll just *flap* down here a minute', *meaning* 'I will take a brief rest here'.

FLAY

> wingless, bloodsucking insect.

FLIER

> basic ingredient of baking, along with eggs.

FLIERS

> blossoms of any type: 'Aren't them *fliers* gorgeous?' is a tribute to the horticultural skills of gardeners, both professional and amateur.

FLY MAN

> *as in* 'He's a real *fly man*', *meaning* 'He is an extremely devious person'.

FOAM

device invented by Alexander Graham Bell
for ease of communication over long or short
distances. The *foam* bill is a cause of dissension
in many homes.

FOOTER

person, usually male, completely unskilled,
especially when washing dishes or carrying out
other domestic chores.

FOOTPAD

strip of tarmac or concrete running along a road
for the better security of pedestrians; also used
for car-parking.

FORTY

as in 'He did it *forty* annoy me', *meaning* 'He
did it especially to upset me'.

FRIZZ

as in 'I'm *frizz*', *meaning* 'I find it exceedingly
cold today'.

FULL

as in 'He wuz *full*', *meaning* 'He had indulged
neither wisely nor well in recreational
chemicals'.

FUR

as in 'Where ye *fur*?', *meaning* 'Where are you going?'

GANDER

as in 'Take a *gander* at this', *meaning* 'Would you mind looking at this and giving me your opinion?'

GET

as in 'Ye wee *get* ye', *meaning* 'You're a small, impudent and possibly illegitimate person'. *Ghost* is occasionally used instead.

also as in '*Get* on ye', *meaning* 'Get dressed this minute ... or else'.

GIMME

as in '*Gimme* that', *meaning* 'Please hand me that item'. The tone of voice is important here: an ordinary conversational tone implies politeness, but the louder the tone, the greater the menace.

GIVE

as in 'Yer Mammy will *give* out to ye',
meaning 'Your mother will forcibly express her
disapproval of your actions'. The expression
is almost obsolete: modern mothers don't give
out.

GNAT

as in 'Yer *gnat*', *meaning* 'I will not under any
circumstances permit you to do that/go there'.

GONE

as in '*Gone* outta that', *meaning* 'I don't
believe your story'.

GORDON

grassy area in front of or behind a house,
sometimes both.

GRAPE

rural Norn Iron speak for an agricultural
implement consisting of four prongs; in urban
circles this is a fork.

GREW

an obsolete term *meaning* greyhound; usually
an unpromising specimen.

GRIND

upper-class Norn Iron speak referring to the earth's surface.

GROAN

as in 'I'm *groan* a few spuds', *meaning* 'I'm making an effort at the good life by cultivating some potatoes in the back garden'.

HA

as in 'See ye at *ha* fate', *meaning* 'I will meet you at half-past eight' (*see also* **fate**).

HANG

as in 'They thew a *hang* run aid', *meaning* 'They hurled a small bomb by hand'.

HAR?

rhetorical question *as in 'Har* are we till do that?', *meaning* 'Are we really expected to carry out such an assignment?'

HARD

as in 'He was *hard* till do the job', *meaning* 'He was engaged, at a fee, to carry out that task'.

The implication here is that the person, and the fee, were a waste.

HATE

as in 'No *hate* the day', *meaning* 'The weather is seasonably cold'.

HAY ROW

as in 'He's a rail *hay row*', *meaning* 'He is a person of considerable bravery'. This is delivered in a sarcastic tone to indicate the direct opposite.

HEADER

as in 'He's a right *header*', *meaning* 'He is an irresponsible person'.

HEAVEN

obsolete rural expression *as in* 'I cud a *heaven*', *meaning* 'I could have had'.

HECKLES

as in 'Something got his *heckles* up', *meaning* 'He was very annoyed about it'.

HENRY'S

as in 'He made a right *Henry's* of it', *meaning* 'He made a complete mess of the job' (*see also* **hard**).

HERBACEOUS

as in 'She has a *herbaceous* hernia', *meaning* 'She suffers from a rupture of the gullet'.

HERE!

wait till I tell you!

HERSELF

significant other in the life of a male person; **Himself** is the male equivalent, though rarely used.

HEX

fissuring of fingertips, heels and toes during cold weather.

HIDING

as in 'He needs a good *hiding*', *meaning* 'His socialisation process would be vastly enhanced by a sharp dose of corporal punishment'.

HIGH

as in '*High high* is at?', *meaning* 'What height is that?'

HIGHER

as in 'He bought it on *higher* purchase', *meaning* 'He purchased the item on the instalment plan'. (*Higher* in this case is a species of Freudian slip.)

HISTORICAL

as in 'She was *historical*', *meaning* 'She reacted in a hysterical manner'.

HONOUR

as in 'She hadn't as much *honour* as would dust a candlestick', *meaning* 'She was scantily clad'.

HORROR SCOPE

feature in newspapers and magazines purporting to foretell the futures of gullible persons by their birth date.

HUM

bad smell.

HUMAN CRY

as in 'There was a *human cry* after him', *meaning* 'People, quite possibly the constabulary, were on the look-out for him'.

HUMP

as in 'He took the *hump*', *meaning* 'He was offended'.

IMPEL

as in 'He's an *impel,* that wee lad', *meaning* 'That child is mischievous to the point of being malicious'.

IMPRISON

as in 'He's *imprison*', *meaning* 'He has been incarcerated for unacceptable behaviour'.

INCENSE

as in 'I cudn't *incense* it intil him', *meaning* 'I was unable to persuade him to see my point of view'.

INCINERATED

as in 'She *incinerated* things about me', *meaning* 'She hinted at disreputable events in my past'.

INK WEST

legal inquiry into circumstances surrounding a death (*see also* **corner**).

INNER

as in 'They were *inner* houses', *meaning* 'They were all at home'.

also 'You *inner* out the night?', *meaning* 'Will you be at home tonight, or have you a social engagement?'

INNER VIEW

meeting with a view to employment.

INSECTS

aromatic substances used to perfume the air.

IRE

period of sixty minutes.

IRON

as in 'It'll take ye an *iron* a bit', *meaning* 'The journey/job will require slightly over an hour'.

ITCH

as in sam-*itch,* snack consisting of two slices of bread with appropriate filling.

Jj

JAB

a task; or employment, either full-time, part-time or temporary.

JACK

as in 'Morrite *Jack*', *meaning* 'I'm doing very nicely; tough about you'.

JAM

as in '*Jam* ember?', *meaning* 'Do you recall?'

JAMMY

as in '*Jammy* bugger', *meaning* 'Fortune appears to have smiled on you ... this time'.

JAR

recreational liquids, such as beer, wine or spirits, but mostly spirits.

JAZZ

large aquatic creature, the subject of a successful Steven Spielberg film and several sequels.

Kk

KEMP

military establishment;

also **kemping** is a popular summer activity.

KEN

tubular metal container used for beer, beans, peas and assorted other consumable items.

KERNEL

senior military officer.

KERRY

as in 'Such a *kerry* on', *meaning* 'Controversy surrounded the event'.

KETCH

to apprehend.

KETTLE

cows, calves, ruminant livestock generally.

KILT

as in 'Ye'll be *kilt* if yer mor or far ketches ye at that', *meaning* 'Dire retribution will follow if your mother or father should spot you doing that'.

KIN

as in '*Kin* ye do that?', *meaning* 'Are you competent to discharge that task?'

KNACK

to summon a householder to the door, especially by use of the **knacker**.

KURD

as in 'He nivvir *kurd*', *meaning* 'He was callously indifferent to the consequences of his actions'.

L

as in 'That's wan *L* of a thing to do/say', *meaning* 'Your action/statement is completely unacceptable'.

LACK

device for securing a door, drawer, etc.;

also as in '*Lack* ah dunno', *meaning* 'I have no answer either'.

LAID

rural Norn Iron speak for sealing material used on church roofs;

also used erroneously for inner core of pencils.

LAIR

as in '*Lair* intil at', *meaning* 'Eat up'.

LANE

as in a *lane* hen, which is a hen capable of laying eggs.

LARD

> *as in* 'He *lard* intil him/it', *meaning* 'He attacked him/his meal with gusto'.

LARRY

> mechanically propelled vehicle for movement of goods by road.

LATTICE

> please allow me, *as in* 'I said *lattice* drive knee said no', *meaning* 'I asked to be permitted to drive but he refused'.

LAVE

> *as in* '*Lave* at air or somebody'll stale it', *meaning* 'It would be safer to deposit that item in this safe place; otherwise, some light-fingered person might appropriate it'.

LAYER

> *as in* '*Layer* intil at', *meaning* 'Enjoy your meal'. (*Leather* and *lair* may also be used in this context.)

LEATHERS

> device used for reaching otherwise inaccessible places, usually on the outside of buildings. The word is singular but appears to be plural.

LEGATE

to run for it.

LENTIL

reinforced concrete slab supporting walls above doors or windows.

LEWD

as in '*Lewd* at', *meaning* 'Please observe that item'.

LION

as in 'I was *lion* for thee days', *meaning* 'My affliction was such that I was confined to bed for three days'.

LIVER

as in 'It doesn't matter to him if I *liver* die', *meaning* 'He is unconcerned about my fate'.

LOOPER

idiot.

LORRY

game of chance, currently known as the lotto.

LUG

as in 'Thick as a bull's *lug*', *meaning* 'He is seriously intellectually challenged'. The origin and connection to a bull's hearing appendage is unknown.

MAGGOT

as in 'Stop acting the *maggot*', *meaning* 'Behave'.

MAIN

as in 'He's a *main* get', *meaning* 'He's a thrifty (*or* tight-fisted) individual'.

MAP

appliance consisting of a handle and a head of absorbent material used in floor cleaning.

MAR?

as in 'Wassa *mar* way you?', *meaning* 'What is the cause of your gloom/distress?'

MARSHAL ARSE

various forms of unarmed combat and self-defence, such as judo or karate.

MASONIC PAINT

paint which is specially formulated for use on cement or concrete surfaces.

MAW

as in '*Maw* rite', *meaning* 'I'm OK'. Often the response to **mar?**

MCCLATCHEY

any tool, the name of which has escaped the user for a moment.

MENDED

as in 'Ye're well *mended*', *meaning* 'You've put on weight'.

MERE

as in '*Mere* you', *meaning* 'Come here at once'.

METER

as in 'I'll *meter* at seven', *meaning* 'She and I will rendezvous at seven o'clock'.

MIDGET

tiny fly.

MINE

as in '*Mine* yer head', *meaning* 'Please duck'.

MINT

period of sixty seconds.

MOMENTUM

souvenir, *as in* 'Nigh I'll present our guest with a wee *momentum* of his visit', *meaning* 'And finally, I would like to give our guest a little reminder of his time with us'.

MORN

Good morning.

MUTTON DUMMY

an obsolete term for tennis shoe, now trainer.

NARK

to complain or nag;

also person noted for these practices.

NECK

as in 'She has some *neck*', *meaning* 'She has a nerve to do/say that'.

NEWT

as in 'tight as a *newt*', *meaning* to be under the influence of recreational liquids. Origin unknown as newts are not known for excessive liquor consumption.

NIBS

as in 'his *Nibs*', *meaning* boss or significant other, invariably male.

NIGH

as in 'Orrite *nigh*?', *meaning* 'Are you better now?'

NODE

as in 'Ah *node* at', *meaning* 'I was already aware of that fact'.

NOGGIN

as in 'Use yer *noggin*', *meaning* 'Think before you act'.

NORWEGIAN

as in 'I'll have *Norwegian*', *meaning* 'I will have another small gin'. The actual drink may be a large one, of course, as in Norn Iron speak 'wee' is used very casually.

NUDE!

I told you so!

OBJECT

as in 'See me, I'm a Brattish *object*', *meaning* 'Please note that I am a taxpaying citizen of the United Kingdom'.

OCH

multi-purpose expression covering all situations and meaning nothing.

ODD

as in 'He's a bit *odd*,' *meaning* 'He is mildly eccentric/completely deranged'.

ODE

as in 'He *ode* it tiller', *meaning* 'It was no more or no less than what she was due after all that she had put up with from him over the years'.

ODOUR

as in 'He *odour* thee quid', *meaning* 'He had never repaid the three pounds he had borrowed from her';

48

also 'He had short-changed her to the tune of three pounds'.

OFFER

as in 'She took it *offer*', *meaning* 'She had the temerity to deprive her of it'. 'It' is usually something of little consequence to the party of the first part, but of greater importance to the second.

OFFICE

as in 'He's *office* head', *meaning* 'He is crazy'. This is a purely subjective view, reflecting the speaker's opinion.

ON

as in 'Yer not *on*', *meaning* 'I refuse to go along with your request/suggestion'.

OR

as in '*or* fella', *meaning* 'third party'.

ORMER

abbreviated form of *Ormer Road*: main and, in parts and on occasion, contested thoroughfare of Belfast.

OWL

literal meaning is *old,* but it may be used to describe items of any age;

also used in greetings *as in* 'Bouchy *owl* han', *meaning* 'Delighted to see you, old friend'.

OYEZ?

Is that a fact?

PACIFICALLY

as in 'I *pacifically* asked for a well-done steak',
meaning 'When placing my order I stressed my
wish for a thoroughly cooked steak'.

PACK

as in 'He gave her a *pack* on the cheek',
meaning 'He kissed her lightly on the cheek'.

PACKET

recess in clothing for the storage of money,
cigarettes and similar useful items.

PAD

footpath; otherwise **crib** pad.

PANE

as in 'Am not *pane* fur at', *meaning* 'I refuse to
hand over good money for that inferior object/
service'; **pen** can also be used.

PAR

electricity supply, usually, but also applied to
political authority; **pyre** is also used.

PARKER

hooded waterproof garment for outdoor wear.

PASSION

downpour in rural area.

PAWN

type of loaf of bread;

also face (disparagingly).

PEAS

as in 'thee *peas* sweet', *meaning* a sofa and two armchairs.

PETITION

lightweight structure subdividing rooms or offices.

PHRASE

as in 'She's going through a *phrase*', *meaning* 'She is experiencing a specific stage in her development'.

PITCHER

portrait, landscape or photograph in public prints.

PLANE

as in 'They were *plane* cords', *meaning* 'They were having a hand of poker'.

PLY

implement for turning over arable land in preparation for crop-sowing, now much valued as garden ornament.

POLES

voting places or surveys of public opinion.

PORTRAY

verse or the art of writing same.

POTATO

as in 'We got a *potato* clock', *meaning* 'We got out of bed at eight am'. Or pm.

PRAYED

as in 'There was a *prayed* holding up the traffic', *meaning* 'A number of persons suitably dressed were walking in the middle of the road behind a band'. This is widespread seasonal activity in Norn Iron.

PUTTER

as in '*Putter* air', *meaning* 'Leave that item over there'.

also invitation to shake hands.

Qq

Q

Christian name; *also* **Cue**, **Shoe** and *Shoey*
(from Shoey McShoe, 19th century Norn
Iron emigrant, founder of Feng Shui, Chinese
furniture-moving corporation).

QUACK

fast.

QUARTER

as in 'It's *quarter* tay six', *meaning* 'It is fifteen
minutes before six o'clock'.

QUICKY

pastry case containing a rich savoury egg
and cream custard, as well as ham or other
ingredients.

QUIRE

organised singing group, especially for classical
or church performances.

Rr

RACK

large stone.

RACKET

firework.

RAISIN

justification (*see also* **rime**).

RAPT

as in 'Ah wan it *rapt*', *meaning* 'Would you mind gift-wrapping that for me?'

RASPATORY

as in 'The dactars said it wuz a *raspatory* problem', *meaning* 'The diagnosis was a breathing difficulty'.

RAY

as in '*Ray* publican', a person favouring presidential-style government over the monarchical variety; anyone believed to hold the above political view.

RECKON

as in 'I didn't *reckon* eyes you', *meaning* 'I didn't know you'.

REEL

as in 'It wuz *reel*', *meaning* 'It was the genuine article';

rail is also used.

RETARD

as in 'He's *retard* thee years nigh', *meaning* 'It is now three years since he gave up work'.

RIFT

sudden expulsion of stomach wind via the mouth.

RIME

as in 'There was no *rime* nor raisin to it', *meaning* 'It made no sense' (*see also* **raisin**).

RIND

as in 'He had a milk *rind*', *meaning* 'He was a milkman'.

RITE

'That's fine then' (*see also* **Yawl**).

ROOD

ill-mannered.

ROSY

variety of wine.

SALAD

as in 'Sink's blacked *salad*', *meaning* 'The sink is completely clogged up'.

SAMARA

the response to the query, 'When zit?', i.e. 'It will take place tomorrow'.

SANDS

area of study involving physics, chemistry or allied subjects.

SANE

a proverb, *as in* 'There's an owl *sane* that many hands make light work'. 'Am *sane*' means 'I take the position that ...'

SARONG

as in '*Sarong* way at?', *meaning* 'What are your objections to that?'

SATURATING?

'What are you eating?'

SAX

gender; *also* copulatory activities. *Sax 'n' valance* describes a particular genre of television and film.

SCARRED

as in 'They *scarred* the country for him', *meaning* 'They searched far and wide for him without success'.

SCOT

as in '*Scot* nothing to do with you', *meaning* 'This does not affect you in any way'.

SCYTHE

point of the compass, opposite north, *as in,* for example, *Scythe* Dine, the southern part of County Down. The *Scythe* of Arland is the Republic of Arland, even though one part of it is further north than Norn Iron.

SEE

as in '*See* me?', a preliminary to an expression of personal opinion: for example, '*See* me, don't lick it', *meaning* 'I don't particularly like it'.

SEX

containers for coal, potatoes, etc.

SHACK

unpleasant surprise.

SHADE

small wooden structure for the storage of garden tools, etc.

SHERRY HALE

fall of hailstones; *sherry* snow, *sherry* rain also common.

SHIRE

light fall of rain;

also device for quick all-over ablution; *also* verb; past tense is **shard**.

SHOE

Christian name (*see also* **Cue** and **Q**).

SHOOTIN

obsolete rural term *as in* 'He wuz wearin' a new *shootin* yalla shoes', *meaning* 'He was dressed in a new suit and wearing shoes which weren't black'.

SIGNED

as in 'I heard the *signed* of a corr', *meaning* 'I heard the sound of an approaching motor vehicle'.

SIN

as in '*Sin* air', *meaning* 'You will find it in there'.

SLOT

as in 'It's *slot* fur at', *meaning* 'It's quite expensive for all that you're getting'.

SMATTER

as in 'What *smatter*?', *meaning* 'What's wrong?'

SNOT

vendor's usual reply to **slot** (above).

SNOW

as in '*Snow* good', *meaning* 'There's no point in pursuing this activity'.

SNUFF

reply to **snot** (above).

SPAT

as in '*Spat* on', *meaning* 'That is exactly right'.

SPIT

as in 'He's the dead *spit* of his far', *meaning* 'His resemblance to his father is quite remarkable'.

SPORT

as in 'They have no *sport*', *meaning* 'Not many people see things their way'.

SQUARE

as in '*Square* crack', *meaning* 'It's most entertaining'.

STERN

as in 'Waddya *stern* at?', *meaning* 'Desist from looking at me in that intent fashion or I will come over there and do you a serious mischief'.

SUMMER

as in 'It's *summer* about here', *meaning* 'The missing item is in this vicinity'.

SWAY

as in 'The train's *sway*', *meaning* 'The locomotive has already departed'.

SWEAT

as in '*Sweat* sotis', *meaning* 'It's raining heavily'.

Tt

TACK

Institute of Further and Higher Education.

TALLY

long established and popular Norn Iron newspaper.

TAMPER

as in 'She was in a *tamper*', *meaning* 'She was angry'. Very angry, probably.

TANNER

pre-decimal coin of small value; purchasing power, if nostalgia is to be believed, equivalent to modern ten-pound note, or more, depending on the amount of recreational chemicals consumed.

TAP

highest level of any structure;

also the '*tap* a the range': the most advanced model.

TAR

defensive structure, of advanced age usually: Scrabo *Tar* is an example; **tyre** is also used.

TARA

obsolete rural term *as in* 'That's *tara*', *meaning* 'That's very bad'.

TARDY

as in 'Am *tardy* at', *meaning* 'I am bored/fed-up/exhausted with this activity'.

TARL

rectangular piece of material used for drying person or dishes; **tile** is also used.

TARRED

as in 'I'm *tarred*', *meaning* 'My exertions have wearied me'.

TEAR

as in 'She wudn't *tear* in the pluckin', *meaning* 'Her make-up fails to hide the fact that she's much more mature than she seems'. A lot more.

TELLER

as in '*Teller* a wanner', *meaning* 'Be so good as to inform that lady I wish to speak to her'.

TERN

> *as in* 'She was *tern* about', *meaning* 'She was rushing here and there in a frenzy of activity'.

THEE

> number coming after two and before four.

THERE THERE THERE

> 'There they are over there.'

THEW

> past tense of the verb **thow**: to hurl.

THROUGH OTHER

> untidy.

TICK AT ONE AIR

> 'I will take that one.'

TIGHTENER

> satisfying meal.

TILLER

> *as in* 'I oney lentit *tiller*', *meaning* 'I did not intend that she should keep it permanently'.

TOADY

obsolete term for very small *as in* 'wee *toady* man', *meaning* a vertically challenged male person.

TOUR

low number *as in* 'Gimme *tour* thee', *meaning* 'I would like a small amount'.

TRIAL

metal tool used by bricklayers and plasterers.

TRICKLER

(i) flag of mainland Arland; (ii) French flag; (iii) any flag of three colours, a fact unknown to critics of (i) above.

TRUSS

as in First *Truss,* leading high-street bank.

TYPEWRITER

obsolete term for office person, usually female, specially trained and employed to operate the keyboard of the forerunner of the computer.

TYPHOON

popular brand of tea.

Uu

ULSTER

as in 'She had a very coarse *ulster* on her leg', *meaning* 'She had a painful condition associated with varicose veins'.

UMBER ELLA

folding device for protection against rain.

UNHORSE

as in '*Unhorse* has only thee legs', *meaning* 'I lost my shirt in a wager on that useless equine quadruped'.

UNMAN

as in '*Unman* wud stale the eye outta yer head', *meaning* 'That fellow is capable of any skulduggery'.

UNMERCIFUL

as in 'There was an *unmerciful* bang', *meaning* 'There was a very loud noise'.

UNSCREW

> *as in* 'Gimme *unscrew*', *meaning* 'Hand me that screw'.

UPDATE

> *as in* 'He's not *update*', *meaning* 'He's not physically capable of that task'.

UPPER

> *as in* '*Upper* down?', query from a lift (or elevator) attendant.

URN

> *as in* 'She doesn't *urn* much', *meaning* 'Her salary is quite low'.

VALANCE

excessive or unjustifiable force.

VALLEY BALL

indoor sport involving ball, net and two teams.

VANE

as in 'She's very *vane*', *meaning* 'She has a high opinion of her looks'.

VERY COARSE

as in 'She was in the hospital with her *very coarse* veins', *meaning* 'She underwent surgery for dilated veins in her lower limbs' (*see also* **ulster**).

VIAL

any one of the letters *a, e, i, o* or *u.*

VOCATIONS

as in 'Americans don't take holidays, they go on *vocations*'.

VOID

as in 'She *void* to get even', *meaning* 'She was determined on revenge'.

VOUCHER

as in 'He will *voucher* for me', *meaning* 'He will attest to my sterling character'.

WAD?

what? *as in* '*Wad* ya want?', *meaning* 'Can I help you?'

WAFER

as in 'Ma *wafer* me tea nigh', *meaning* 'I'm taking my tea break now'.

WAN

first number, *as in* '*wan,* two, thee'.

WAR

as in 'Gissa glassa *war*', *meaning* 'Can I have a drink of water, please?'

WARM

as in 'Ah'll *warm* yer ear', *meaning* 'I will adminster a cuff on the ear'.

WARREN

as in '*Warren* diffs here', *meaning* 'We have encountered a problem/complication at this point'.

WATT?

as in 'N-*watt*?', *meaning* 'What happened next?'

WAY ON

'Your request is denied.'

WEAR

as in '*Wear* away nigh', *meaning* 'We are just about to leave'.

WEE

multi-purpose, all-embracing and misleading expression, *as in* '*wee* injection/operation/job'. 'Take a *wee* seat' conveys nothing about the size of the chair but expresses a vague suggestion that you will not be kept waiting long. There is, of course, no substance whatever to this.

WEIR

as in 'Ah wanna *weir* wan', *meaning* 'Can I have this in a smaller size, please?'

WEIR THAT

'I don't believe you.'

WINDY

opening in a wall, filled with glass, enabling those inside to see out, those outside to look in, and for light to pass in either direction.

WIRE

as in 'The *wires* shakkin', *meaning* 'Meteorological conditions are poor'.

WISE

instruction to a third party to get real.

WOBBLER

as in 'She thew a *wobbler*', *meaning* 'She lost her temper'.

WOE!

'That's (far) enough.'

WORD

as in '*Word ye* get at?', *meaning* 'How did you come into possession of that item?'

WORSEN

as in 'Yer *worsen* a wane', *meaning* 'Your behaviour is even more childish than that of a child'.

WROUGHT

obsolete rural term *as in* 'He *wrought* all his days', *meaning* 'He was never on the dole even once'.

X-CAPED

as in 'They *x-caped*', *meaning* 'They eluded their captors'.

X-ERCISE

statutory body which collects VAT.

X-YLEM

as in 'Them *x-ylem* seekers is everywhere nigh', *meaning* 'The number of economic migrants in this country is rising steadily'.

YALE

as in '*Yale* take a wee drink?', *meaning* 'Can I offer you a liquid refreshment?'

YAM

I am.

YAWL

as in '*Yawl* rite air?', *meaning* 'Is everything to your satisfaction?'

also used simply as a greeting; in a retail or similar establishment it means 'Can I help you?' (In this case it also implies 'I've got my eye on you.') (*see also* **yis**)

YIS

the answer in the affirmative to **yawl**.

YONDER

as in '*Yonder* at?', *meaning* 'Are you underneath that vehicle/pile of rubble?'

YUMAN BEAN

member of the human race.

YUP

as in '*Yup* yit?', *meaning* 'Are you going to get out of bed today at all?' The reply (usually a lie) is **mup**; **yam** is also used.

YURT

as in '*Yurt* yerself?', *meaning* 'Are you all right?'

ZETA

as in 'See him? *Zeta* a whole loaf!', *meaning* 'He has a voracious appetite'.

ZING

as in 'There's a bitta *zing* way at', *meaning* 'There's a kick in that'.

ZIT

as in 'When zit?', *meaning* 'When will it happen?'

ZIZZ

as in bitta *zizz*: a nap.

ZYM

It's him.